My first I can draw

Follow the simple steps to
learn how to draw lots of charming
characters and cool vehicles.

•

Tear out the practice pages
to perfect your pictures before
drawing them in the scenes.

Inside this book there are:

Creepy crawlies
Wild animals
Farmyard friends

Cuddly creatures
Sea life
Things that go

make
believe
ideas

Drawing **shapes**

The characters and vehicles in this book are constructed using some basic shapes. Try drawing them first, and you will be ready to go!

Spiral

Start in the middle and draw out.

Square

Draw four equal, straight sides.

Rectangle

Draw two short, straight sides and two long, straight sides.

Try drawing here . . . .

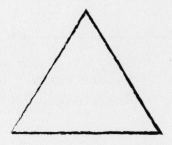

Triangle 1

Draw three equal, straight sides.

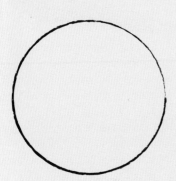

Triangle 2

Draw two long, straight sides and one short, straight side.

Circle

Draw one round side that joins.

Semicircle

Draw half a circle with one straight side.

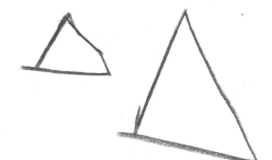

Spotted ladybugs

1 Draw a circle for the head and a semicircle for the body.

2 Add two lines for the antennae.

Try drawing your own . . .

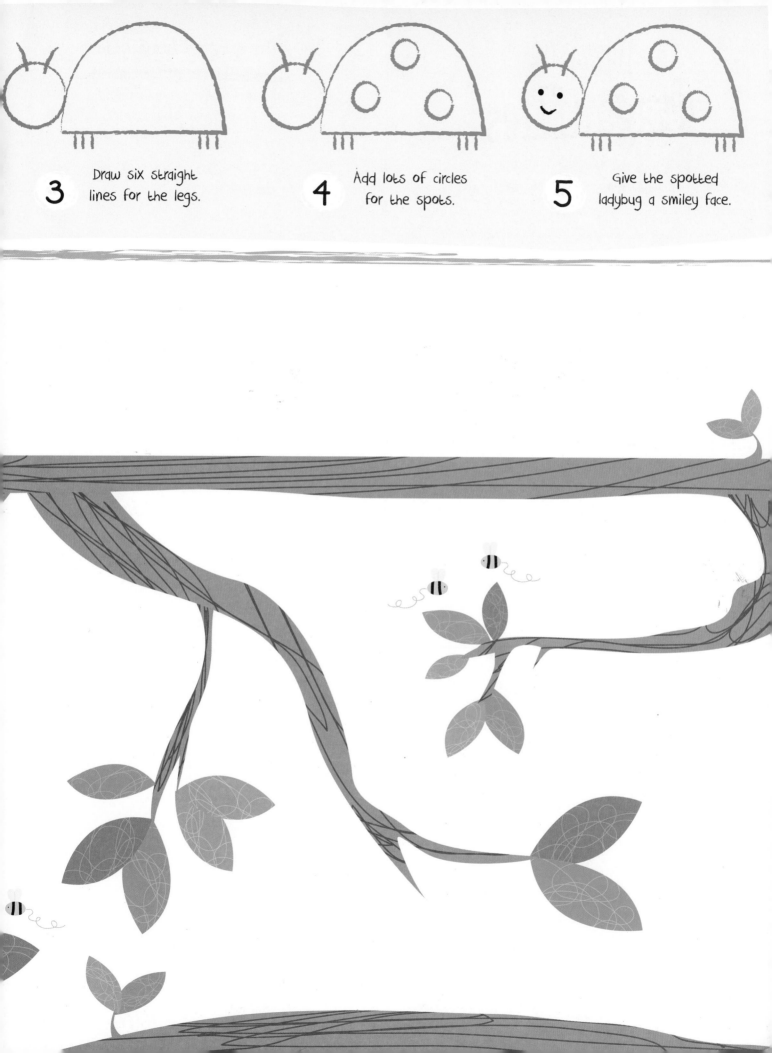

3 Draw six straight lines for the legs.

4 Add lots of circles for the spots.

5 Give the spotted ladybug a smiley face.

Dazzling
dragonflies

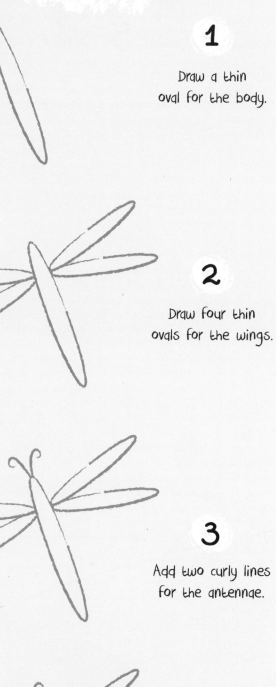

1

Draw a thin
oval for the body.

2

Draw four thin
ovals for the wings.

3

Add two curly lines
for the antennae.

4

Give the dragonfly
two eyes.

Fantastic **frogs**

1 Draw the body.

2 Add two circles for the eyes.

Try drawing your own . . .

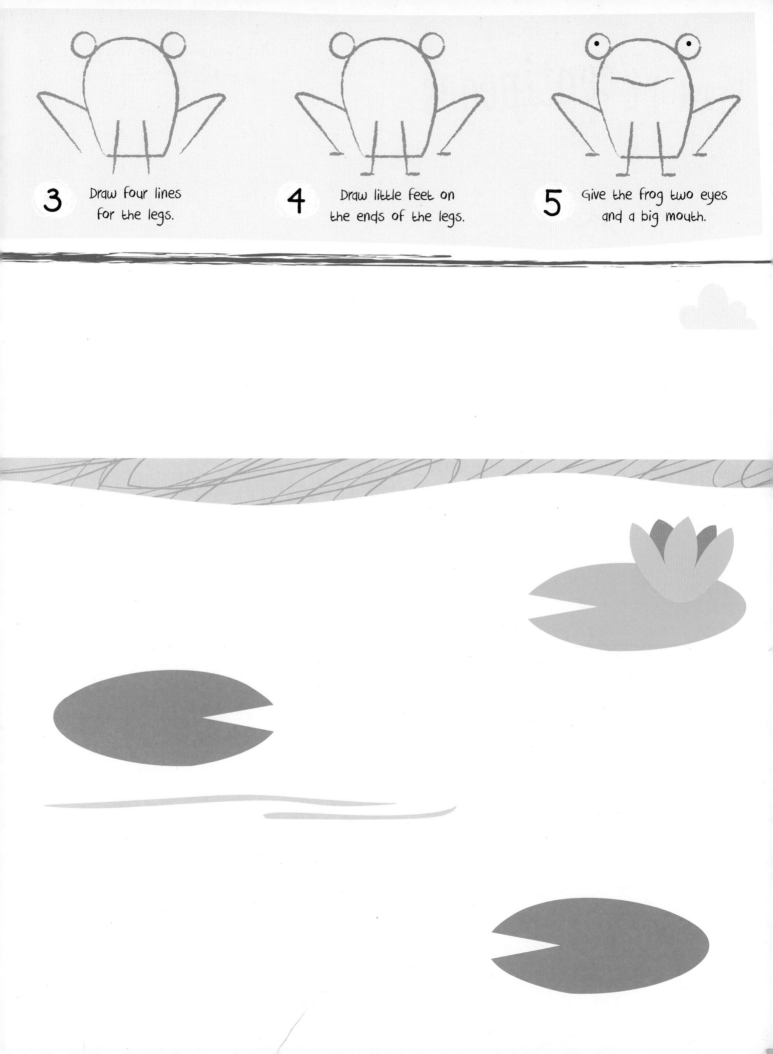

3 Draw four lines for the legs.

4 Draw little feet on the ends of the legs.

5 Give the frog two eyes and a big mouth.

Crawling **centipedes**

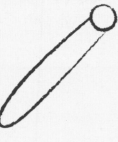

1

Draw a circle for the head and add a long body.

2

Add two back legs.

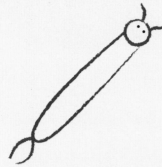

3

Give the centipede two eyes and two antennae.

4

Draw lots of short lines for the legs.

Green grasshoppers

1 Draw an oval for the head and a semicircle for the body.

2 Add two lines for the antennae.

Try drawing your own . . . .

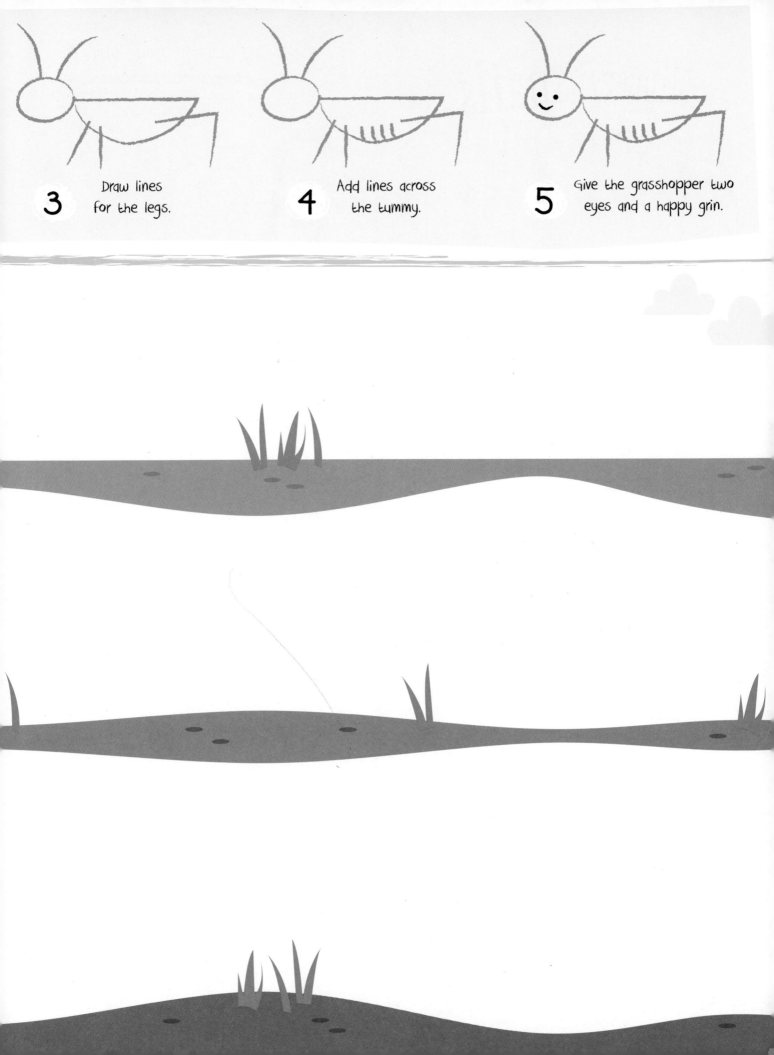

3 Draw lines for the legs.

4 Add lines across the tummy.

5 Give the grasshopper two eyes and a happy grin.

Slippery **snails**

Try drawing your own . . .

1

Draw the body.

2

Draw a circle for
the shell and
add a slimy tail.

3

Draw a spiral
in the shell.

4

Give the snail
two antennae, two
eyes, and
a gooey grin.

Silly slugs

1 Draw the body.

2 Add a tail.

Try drawing your own . . .

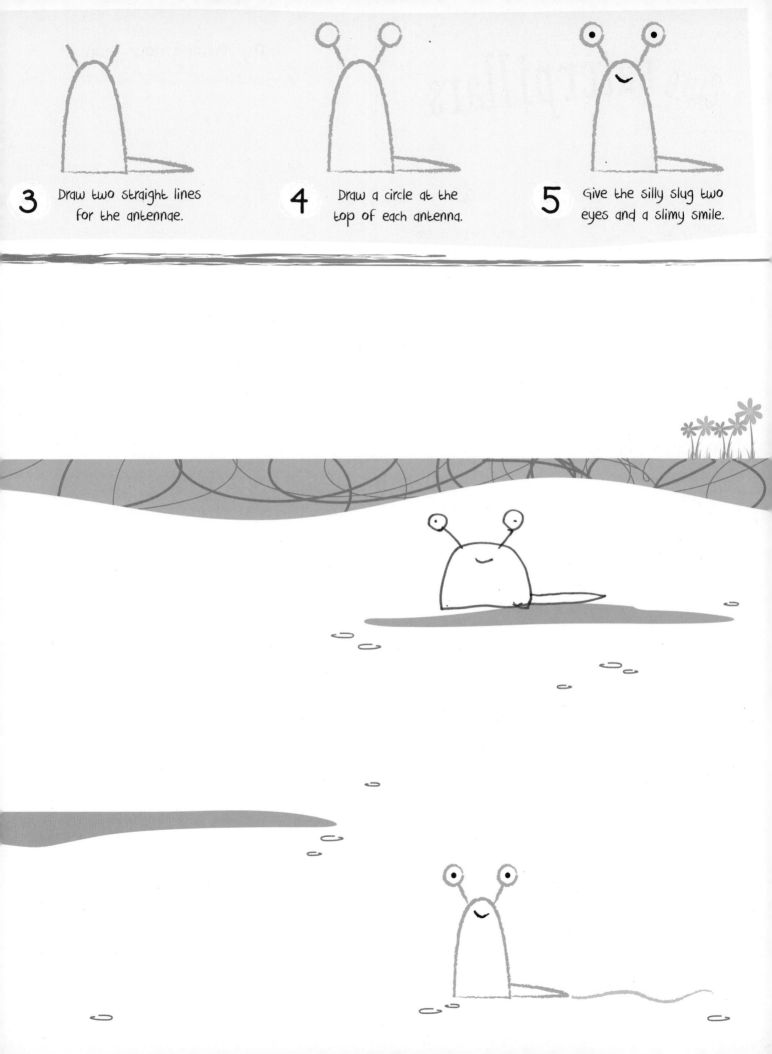

3 Draw two straight lines for the antennae.

4 Draw a circle at the top of each antenna.

5 Give the silly slug two eyes and a slimy smile.

Cute **caterpillars**

1

Draw three circles
for the body.

2

Draw six lines
for the legs.

3

Add a circle
for the head.

4

Give the caterpillar
a cute face and
two antennae.

Tiny tadpoles

1

Draw an oval for the head.

2

Draw a wiggly line for the tail.

3

Add two curved lines to finish the tail.

4

Give the tiny tadpole a happy face.

Try drawing your own . . .

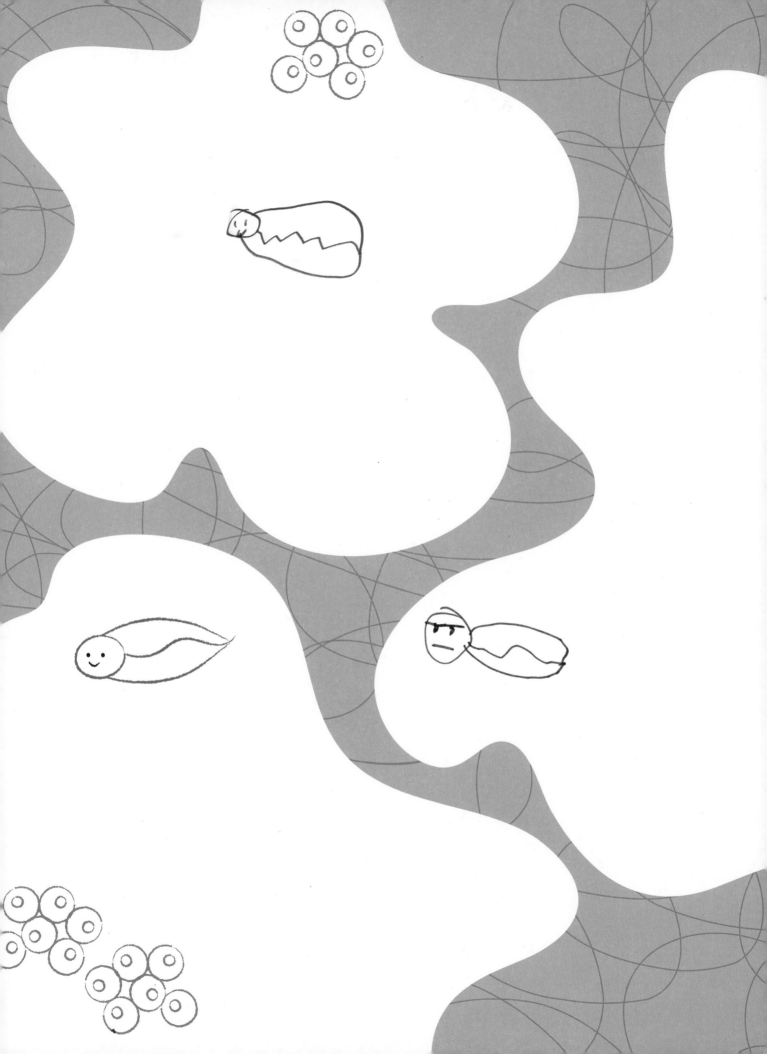

Groovy geckos

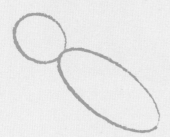

1
Draw a circle for the head and an oval for the body.

2
Add curved lines for the legs and tail.

3
Give the gecko two eyes and four feet for running over rocks.

Try drawing your own . . .

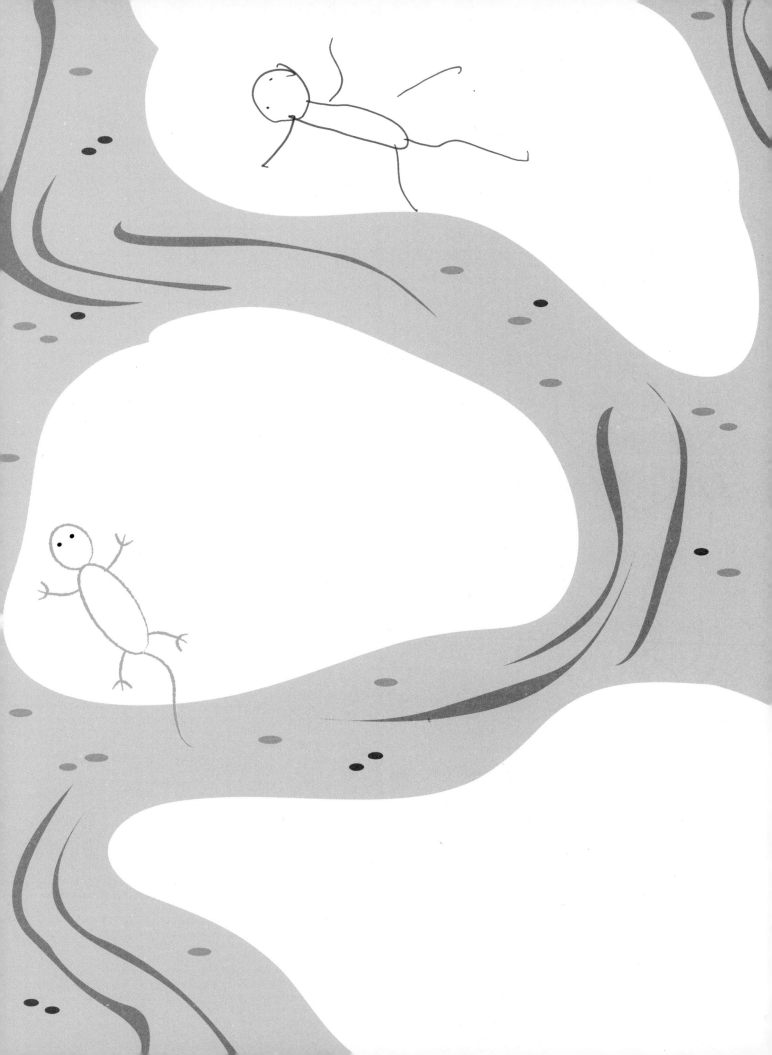

Terrifying
tarantulas

Try drawing your own . . .

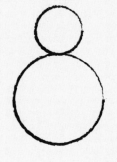

1

Draw a small circle
for the head and
a big circle for
the body.

2

Add eight long lines
for the legs.

3

Draw two
short lines for
the pincers.

4

Give the tarantula
two terrifying eyes
and stripes.

Slithering cobras

1 Draw a circle for the head.

2 Add the long body.

Try drawing your own . . .

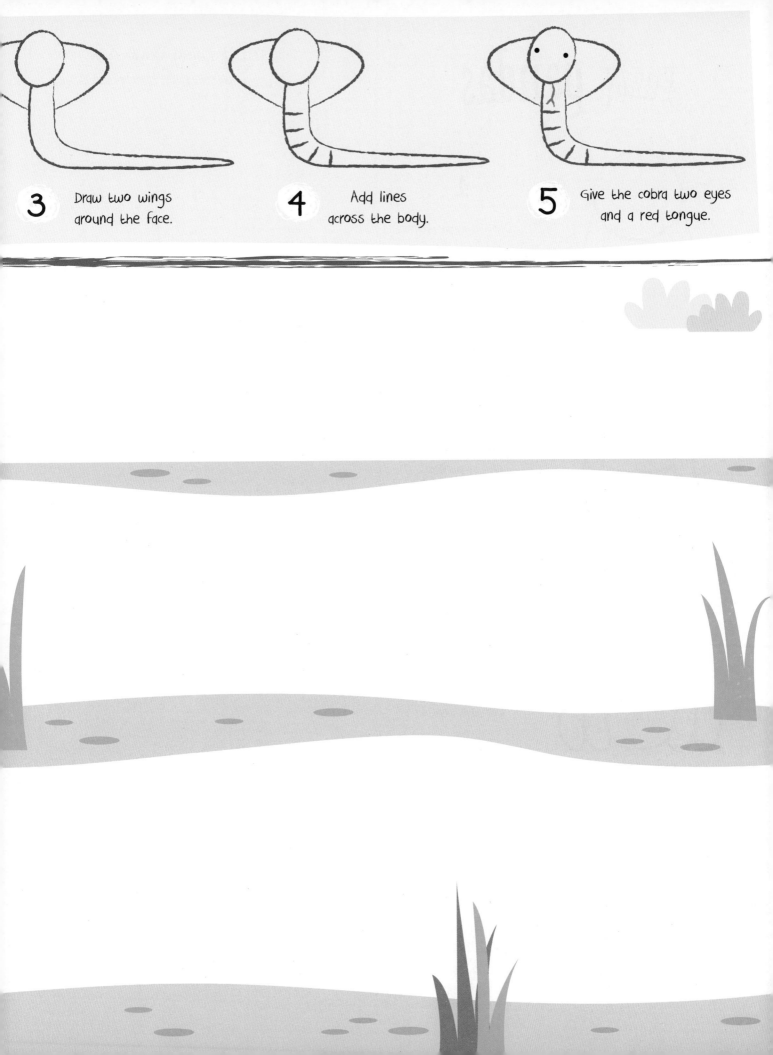

3 Draw two wings around the face.

4 Add lines across the body.

5 Give the cobra two eyes and a red tongue.

Fuzzy **pandas**

1

Draw a circle for the head and add two long arms.

2

Add the tummy and a stripe. Draw two semicircles for the ears.

3

Add two ovals for the feet.

4

Give the playful panda a fuzzy face with two circles for the eye patches.

Try drawing your own . . .

Leaping lions

1

Draw a circle for the head and a curly mane.

2

Add the body and two semicircles for the ears.

3

Draw four legs and a tail.

4

Give the lion a fierce face and a fluffy tail.

Enormous **elephants**

1

Draw a rectangle for the body.

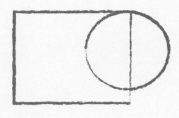

2

Draw a circle across the rectangle to make the head and ear.

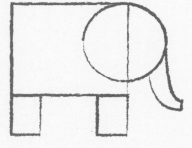

3

Add two rectangles for the legs and add a long trunk.

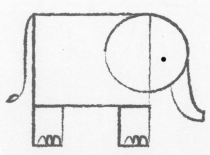

4

Give the elephant a long tail, an eye, and some toenails.

Clever camels

1 Draw an oval for the body.

2 Draw a semicircle for the hump.

Try drawing your own . . .

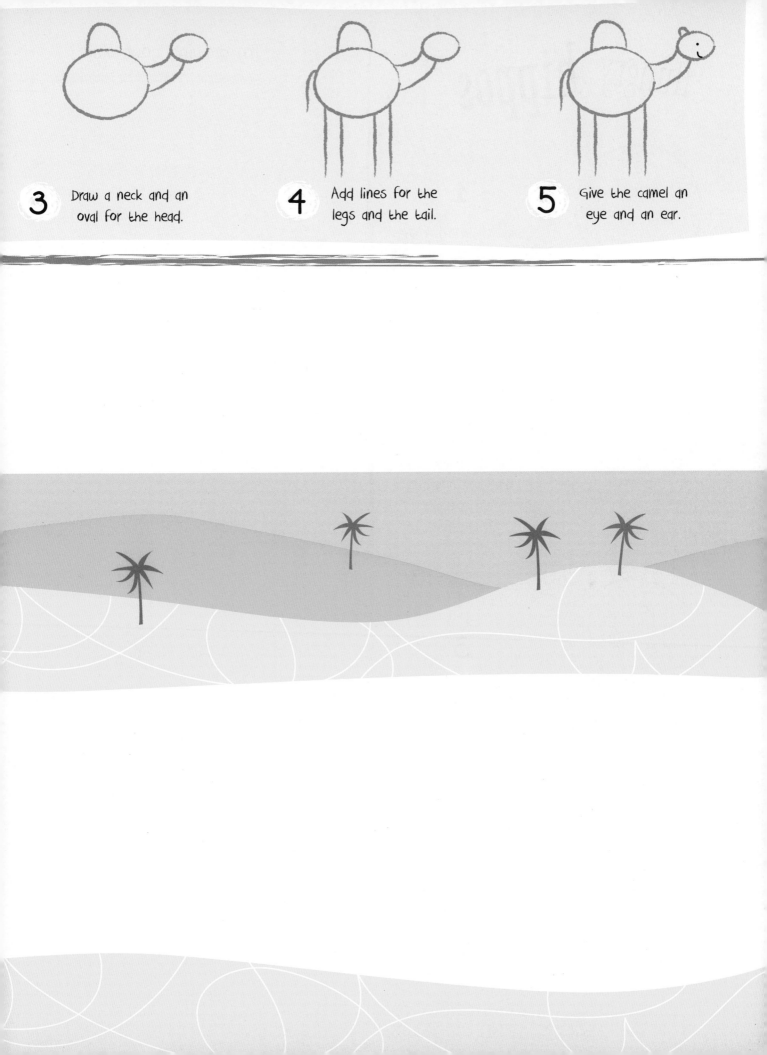

3 Draw a neck and an oval for the head.

4 Add lines for the legs and the tail.

5 Give the camel an eye and an ear.

Hungry **hippos**

1

Draw a circle for the
body and add two legs.

2

Draw an oval
for the nose and
add two nostrils.
Add toenails
to the feet.

3

Draw a semicircle
for the head.

4

Give the happy
hippo two eyes and
two oval ears.

Cheerful **cheetahs**

1

Draw a head and a body.

2

Add two semicircles for the ears and a wiggly line for the tail.

3

Give the cheetah two eyes and two dark stripes. Add four lines for the legs.

4

Add a nose and a mouth. Draw lots of fuzzy spots.

Try drawing your own . . .

Goofy gorillas

1 Draw a face and two arms.

2 Add a semicircle for the head and draw two hands.

Try drawing your own . . .

3 Finish the body and draw two back legs.

4 Draw two ears.

5 Give the gorilla a happy face.

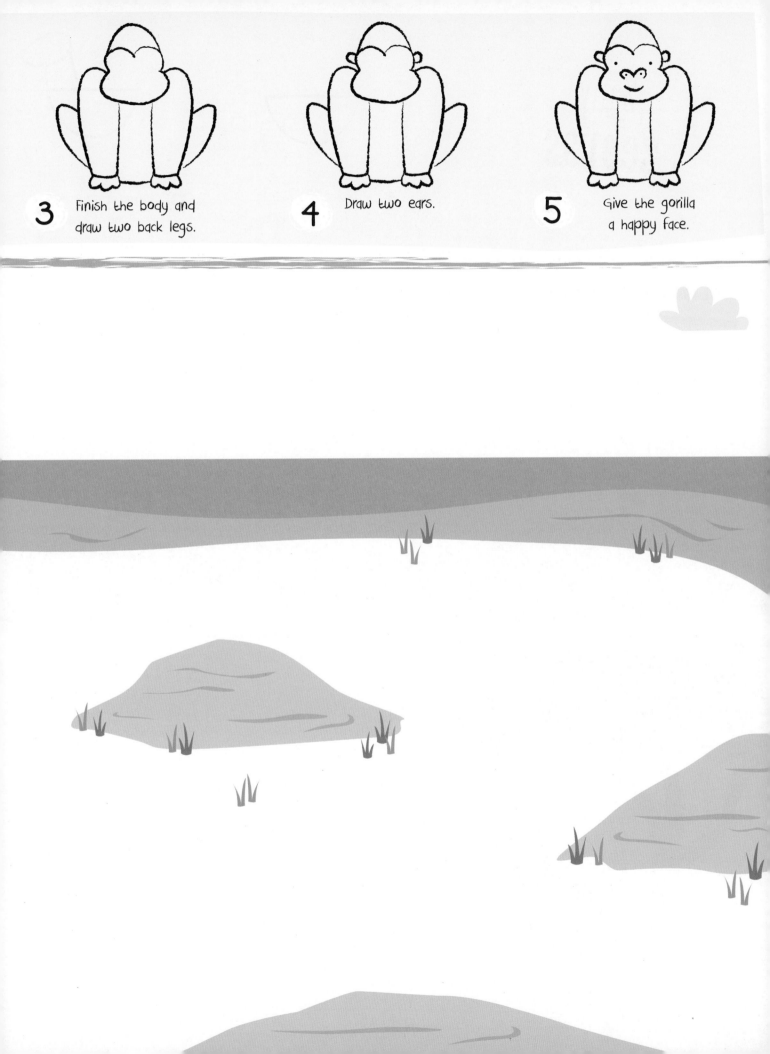

Zany zebras

1 Draw a semicircle for the body.

2 Add a long neck and a head.

Try drawing your own . . .

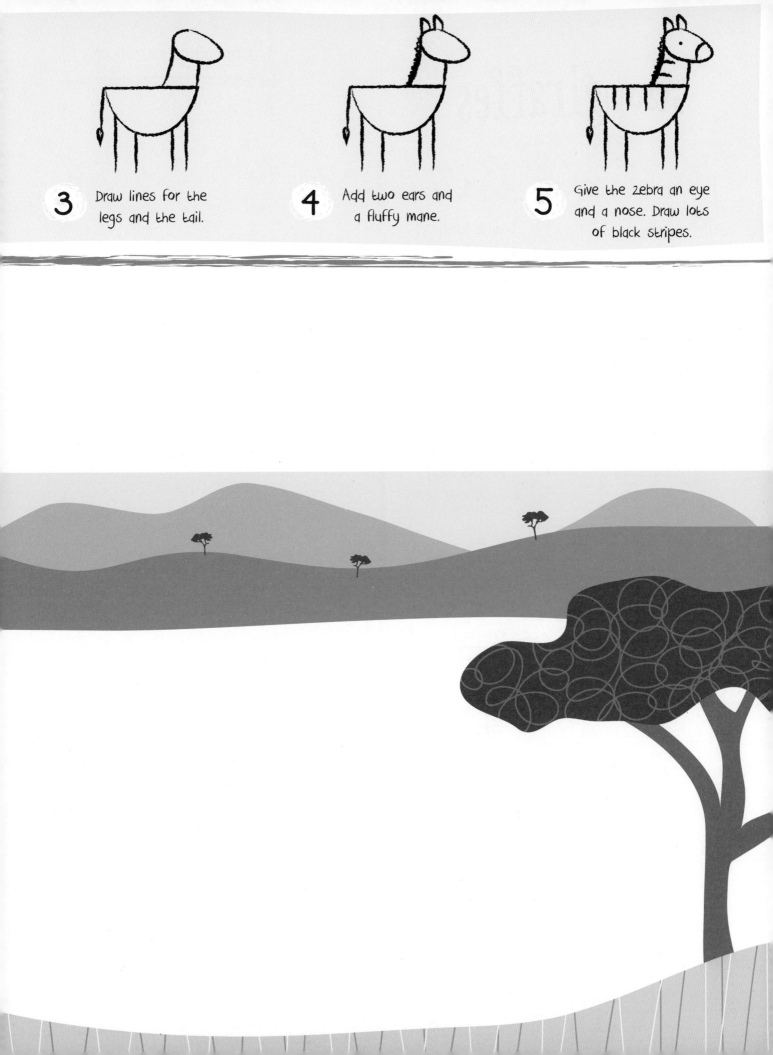

3 Draw lines for the legs and the tail.

4 Add two ears and a fluffy mane.

5 Give the zebra an eye and a nose. Draw lots of black stripes.

Giant giraffes

1
Draw a head and a very long neck.

2
Draw a rectangle for the body and add two ears.

3
Add lines for the legs and the tail. Draw two horns.

4
Give the giant giraffe two eyes and two nostrils. Add lots of spots.

Try drawing your own . . .

Grizzly bears

1 Draw the head and the body.

2 Add two semicircles for the ears and draw a small tail.

Try drawing your own . . .

3 Draw four lines for the legs.

4 Add a circle for the snout.

5 Give the grizzly bear a happy face.

Muddy rhinos

1 Draw a rectangle for the body and add the head.

2 Add two ears and a tail.

Try drawing your own . . .

3 Draw two rectangles for the legs.

4 Add a horn on the rhino's nose.

5 Give the rhino two eyes and nostrils and add a smile.

Hissing **snakes**

1

Draw a long, wiggly body.

2

Add a head and a forked tongue.

3

Draw stripes at the end of the tail.

4

Give the slithery snake patterned scales.

Try drawing your own . . .

Grazing **goats**

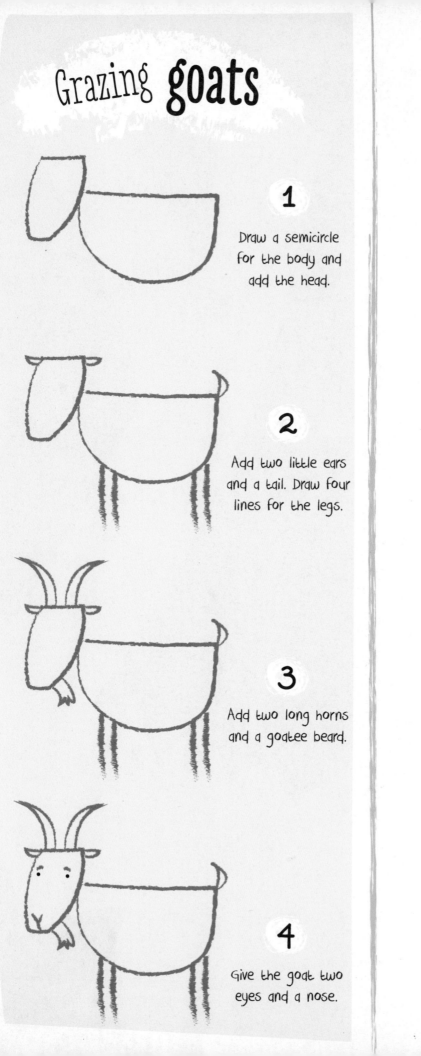

1

Draw a semicircle for the body and add the head.

2

Add two little ears and a tail. Draw four lines for the legs.

3

Add two long horns and a goatee beard.

4

Give the goat two eyes and a nose.

Try drawing your own . . .

Lively **llamas**

1

Draw a big oval
for the body
and a small oval
for the head.

2

Add a long neck
and two little ears.

3

Draw four lines for
the legs and add
a fluffy tail.

4

Give the llama
two eyes and
a sweet nose.

Rowdy roosters

1 Draw a semicircle for the body and add the head.

2 Add a wing.

Try drawing your own . . .

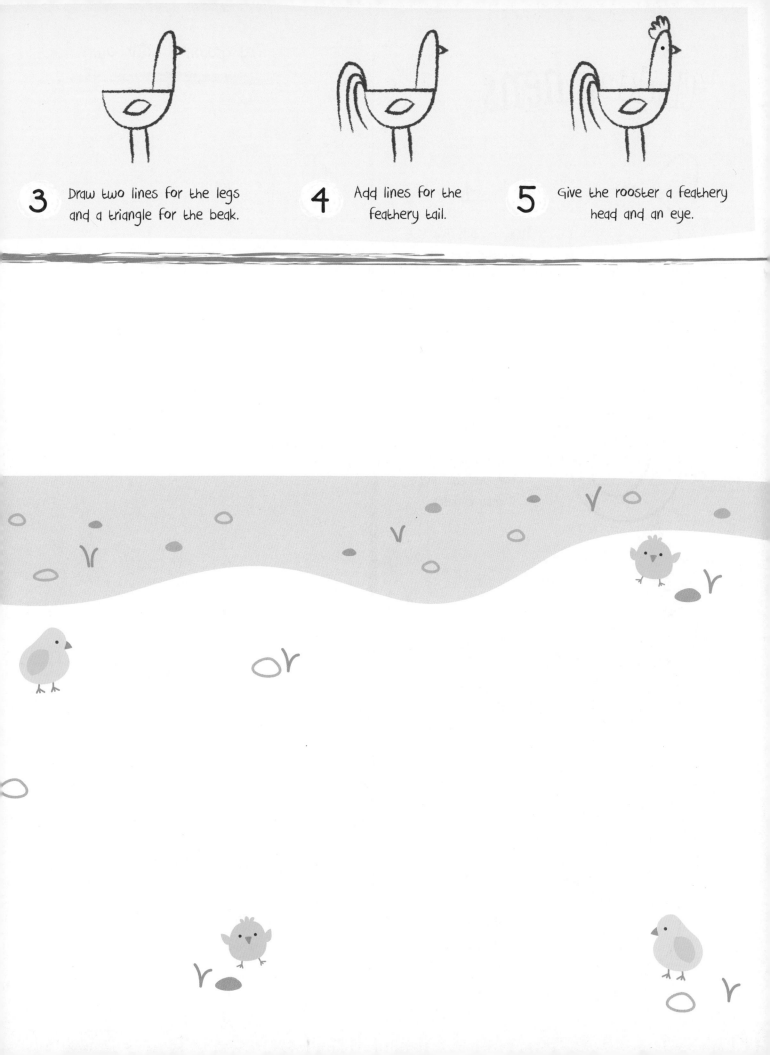

3 Draw two lines for the legs and a triangle for the beak.

4 Add lines for the feathery tail.

5 Give the rooster a feathery head and an eye.

Clucking **hens**

1

Draw a circle for the body and add a head.

2

Add a triangle for the tail and draw a wing.

3

Draw two lines for the legs and a triangle for the beak.

4

Give the hen a feathery head and an eye.

Try drawing your own . . .

Fluffy **sheep**

1

Draw a fluffy body.

2

Add four lines
for the legs.

3

Draw an oval
for the head and
add two ears.

4

Give the sheep
a cute face.

Try drawing your own . . .

Oinking **pigs**

1

Draw a circle for the body.

2

Add two little legs.

3

Draw two triangles for the ears and add a curly tail.

4

Give the muddy pig two eyes and a big, pink snout.

Try drawing your own . . .

Mooing COWS

1 Draw a body. Add a head and draw an oval for the nose.

2 Draw two lines for the leg and add two little ears.

Try drawing your own . . . .

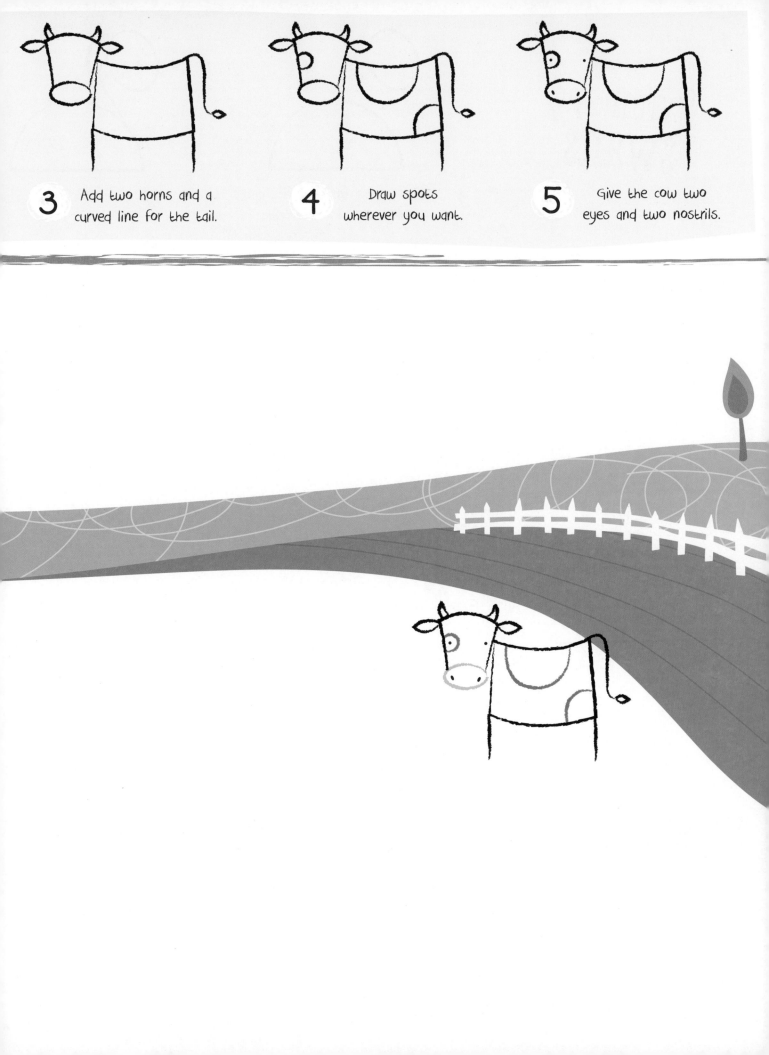

3 Add two horns and a curved line for the tail.

4 Draw spots wherever you want.

5 Give the cow two eyes and two nostrils.

Swimming swans

1 Draw an oval for the head and a semicircle for the body.

2 Add a long, curved neck.

Try drawing your own . . .

3 Draw a tail and a beak.

4 Add a wing.

5 Give the swimming swan an eye.

Happy horses

1

Draw the head
and a neck.

2

Add an oval
for the body and
draw two ears.

3

Draw lines for
the legs and tail.

4

Give the happy
horse a face and
a shaggy mane.

Try drawing your own . . .

Feathery turkeys

1 Draw a circle for the head and add a neck.

2 Draw an oval for the body and add the bushy tail.

Try drawing your own . . .

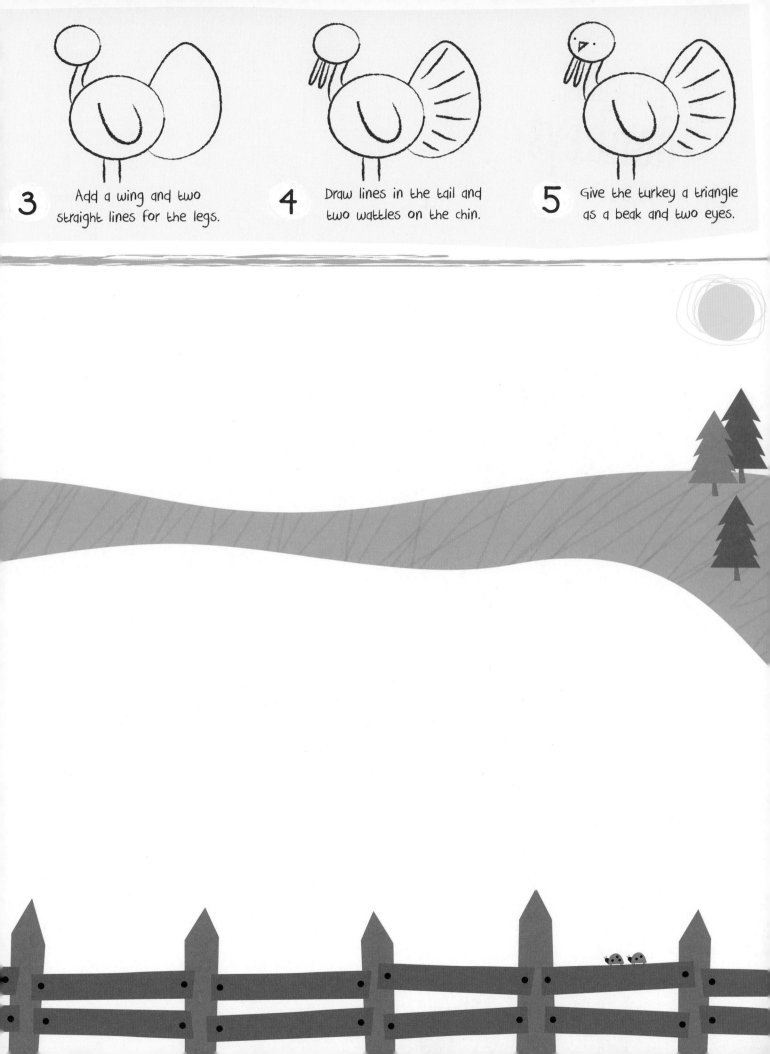

3 Add a wing and two straight lines for the legs.

4 Draw lines in the tail and two wattles on the chin.

5 Give the turkey a triangle as a beak and two eyes.

Adorable donkeys

1 Draw a rectangle for the body.

2 Add four straight lines for the legs.

Try drawing your own . . .

3 Draw a head and add a line for the neck.

4 Add two big ears and a line for the tail.

5 Give the donkey a face.

Bumbling baby bears

1 Draw a circle for the head and add two long arms.

2 Add two semicircles for the ears and draw the tummy.

Try drawing your own . . .

3 Draw two ovals for the feet.

4 Add a cute face.

5 Give the bear two rosy cheeks!

Playful **pugs**

1

Draw the head
and body.

2

Add two ears
and a tail.

3

Draw four
little legs.

4

Give the pug
a face with
a cute nose!

Try drawing your own . . .

Gentle **gerbils**

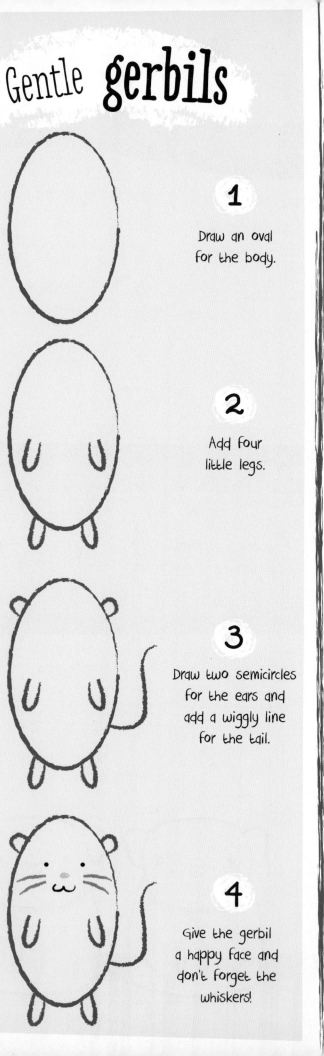

1

Draw an oval for the body.

2

Add four little legs.

3

Draw two semicircles for the ears and add a wiggly line for the tail.

4

Give the gerbil a happy face and don't forget the whiskers!

Try drawing your own . . .

Perfect **puppies**

1 Draw an oval for the head and add the body.

2 Add two floppy ears.

Try drawing your own . . .

3 Draw two front paws.

4 Add two ovals for the back feet.

5 Give the puppy a face with a wet nose.

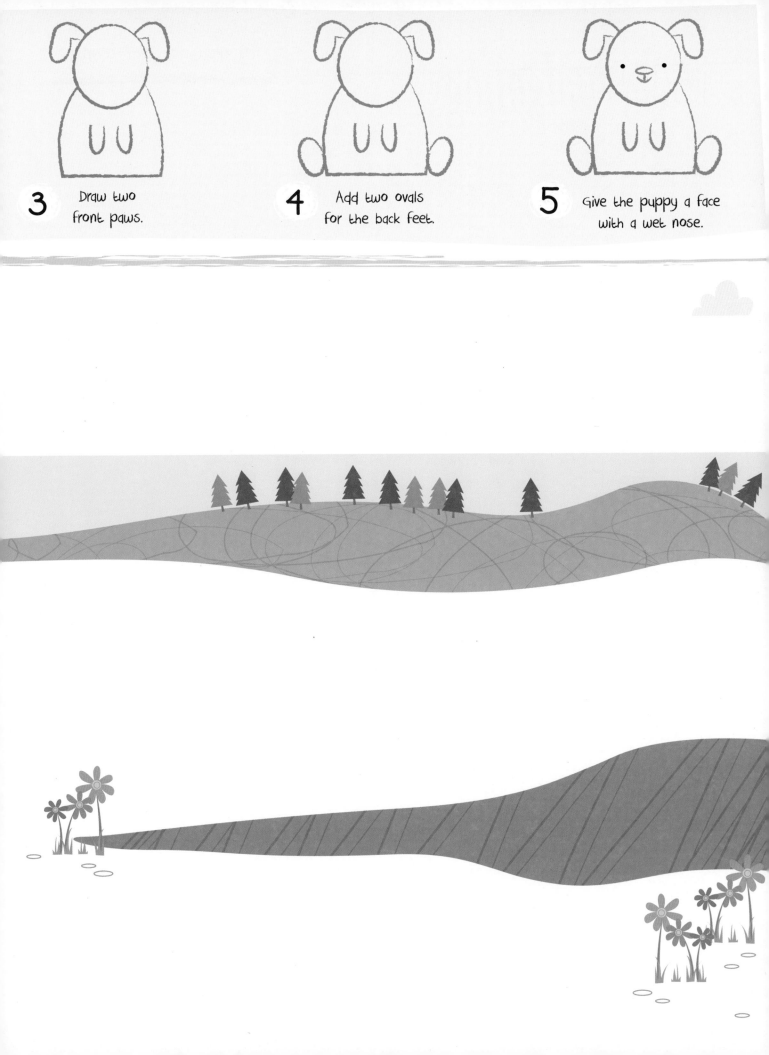

Prickly **hedgehogs**

Try drawing your own . . . .

1

Draw
the body.

2

Add the legs
and an ear.

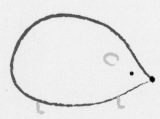

3

Give the hedgehog
an eye and a nose.

4

Draw lots of little
lines for the
hedgehog's prickles.

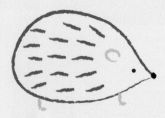

Bright budgies

1 Draw an oval for the head and add the body.

2 Add two feathery wings.

Try drawing your own . . .

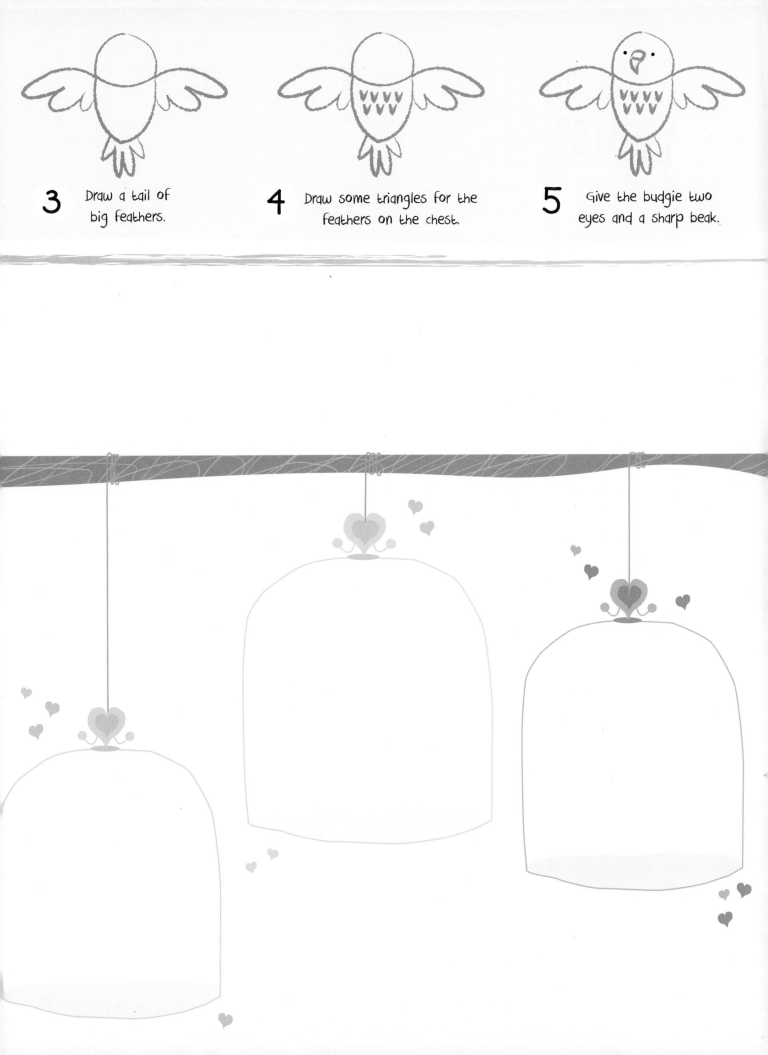

3 Draw a tail of big feathers.

4 Draw some triangles for the feathers on the chest.

5 Give the budgie two eyes and a sharp beak.

Prancing ponies

1 Draw the head and neck.

2 Add two ears and part of a rectangle for the body.

Try drawing your own . . .

3 Draw four lines for the legs.

4 Add a shaggy mane and a curved line for the tail.

5 Give the pony two eyes and a big nose.

Lovely labradors

1

Draw a head and a circle for the nose.

2

Add the body and two ears.

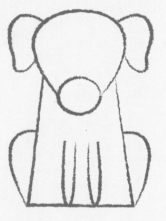

3

Draw two front paws and two back legs.

4

Give the labrador a cute face and a wiggly line for the tail.

Try drawing your own . . .

Bouncing **bunnies**

1

Draw a circle for the head and add a body.

2

Add two big ears and two front paws.

3

Draw a circle for the tail.

4

Give the bunny a happy face.

Huggable hamsters

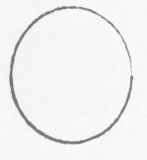

1

Draw an oval
for the body.

2

Add two semicircles
for the ears.

3

Give the hamster
a sweet face.

4

Draw two
front paws and
two back paws.

Try drawing your own . . .

Cuddly kittens

1 Draw an oval head and a body.

2 Add two triangles for the ears.

Try drawing your own . . . .

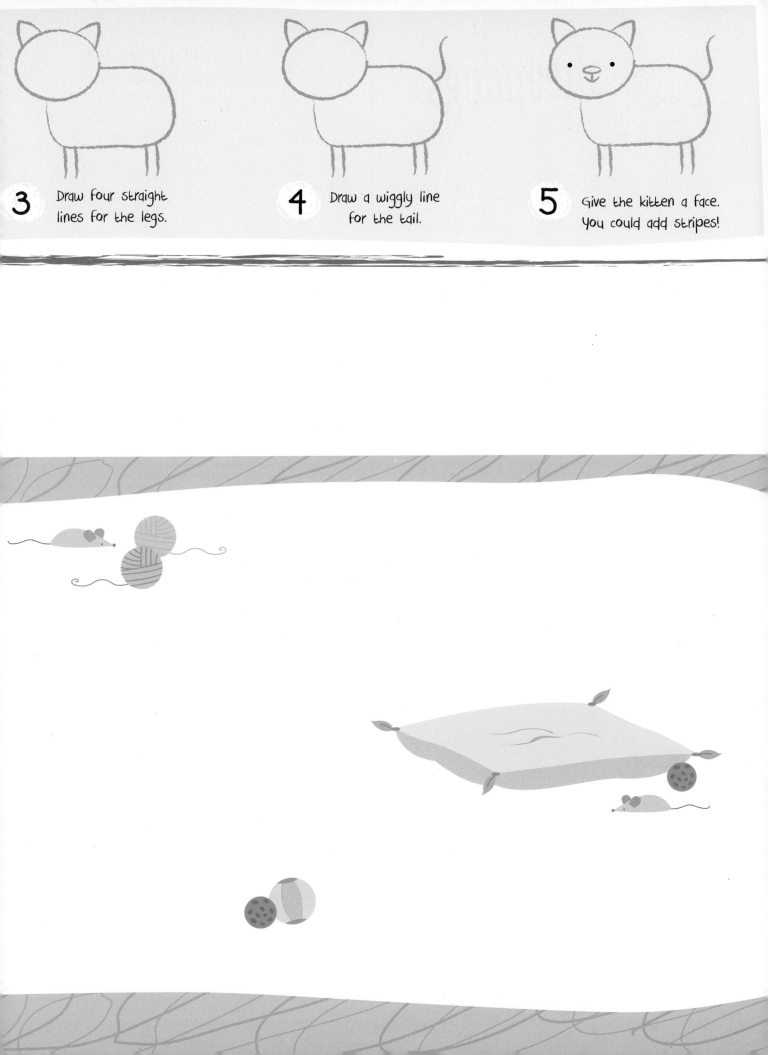

3 Draw four straight lines for the legs.

4 Draw a wiggly line for the tail.

5 Give the kitten a face. You could add stripes!

Shaggy sheepdogs

Try drawing your own . . .

1

Draw a circle
for the head and
add a furry chest.

2

Add two ears and
two front legs.

3

Draw two back legs.

4

Give the
sheepdog a
shaggy face and
a little tongue.

Daring dolphins

1 Draw a semicircle for the body and add a nose.

2 Add a tail with two fins.

Try drawing your own . . .

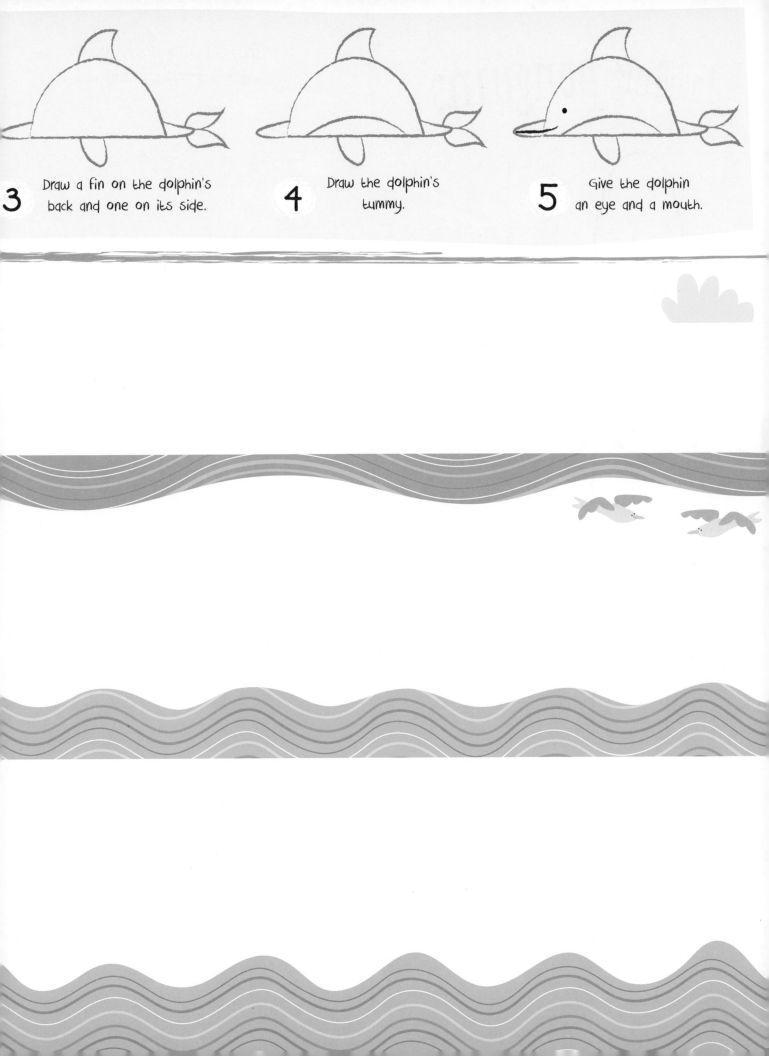

3 Draw a fin on the dolphin's back and one on its side.

4 Draw the dolphin's tummy.

5 Give the dolphin an eye and a mouth.

Paddling **penguins**

1

Draw the body.

2

Add two triangles for the wings.

3

Draw the tummy and two feet.

4

Give the penguin two eyes and a triangle for the beak.

Try drawing your own . . .

Snappy sharks

1 Draw a semicircle for the body.

2 Draw two triangles for the fins.

Try drawing your own . . .

3 Draw a big triangle for the back fin.

4 Draw lines for the gills.

5 Give the snappy shark an eye and smile.

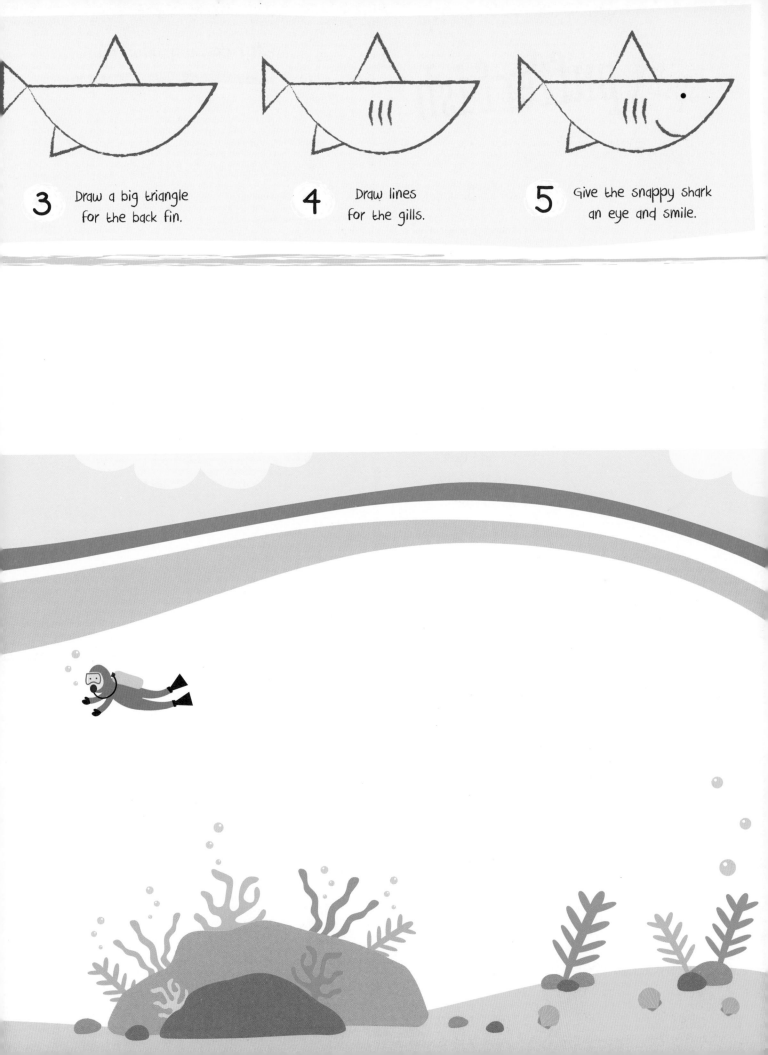

Spiky **pufferfish**

1

Draw a big circle for the body.

2

Add two triangles for the fins.

3

Draw lines sticking out of the body for the spikes.

4

Give the pufferfish a smiley face.

Try drawing your own . . .

Waddling **walrus**

1

Draw a circle for the head and part of a triangle for the body.

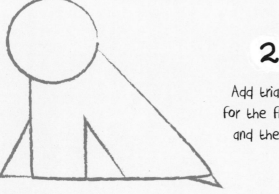

2

Add triangles for the flippers and the tail.

3

Draw two triangles for the tusks and a line across the face for the snout.

4

Give the walrus two eyes and a nose. Draw some long whiskers.

Try drawing your own . . . .

Blue whales

1 Draw a semicircle for the body.

2 Add a curved line for the tail.

Try drawing your own . . .

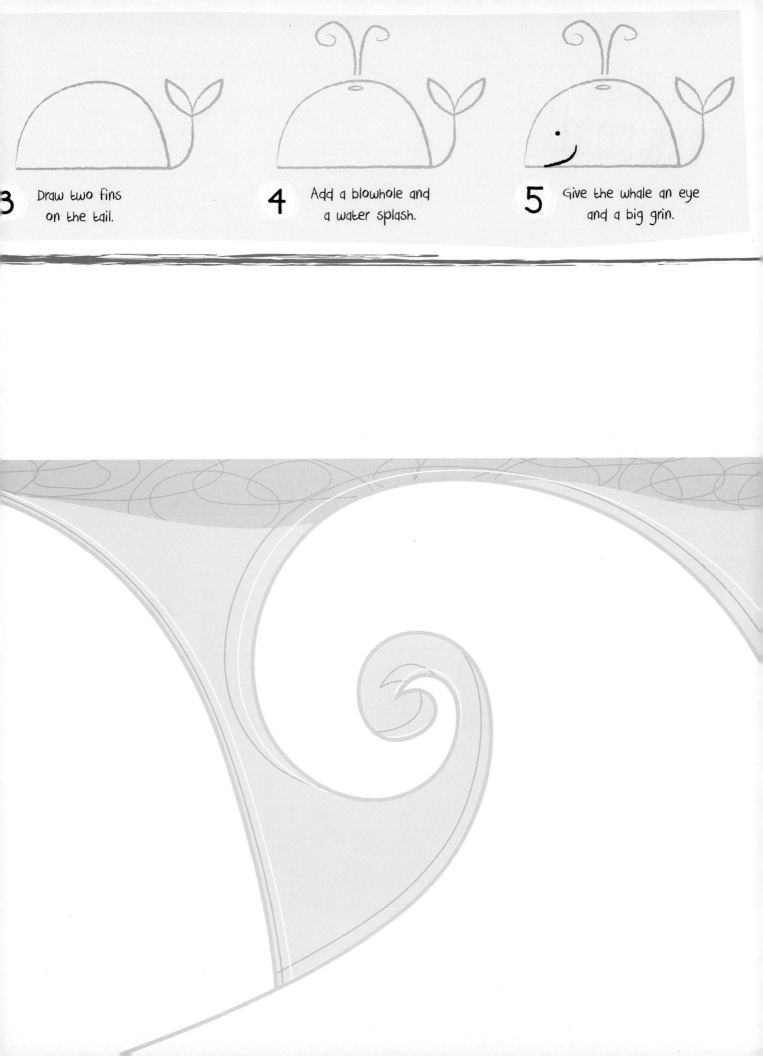

3 Draw two fins on the tail.

4 Add a blowhole and a water splash.

5 Give the whale an eye and a big grin.

Slimy sea snails

1 Draw a semicircle for the shell.

2 Add the head.

Try drawing your own . . .

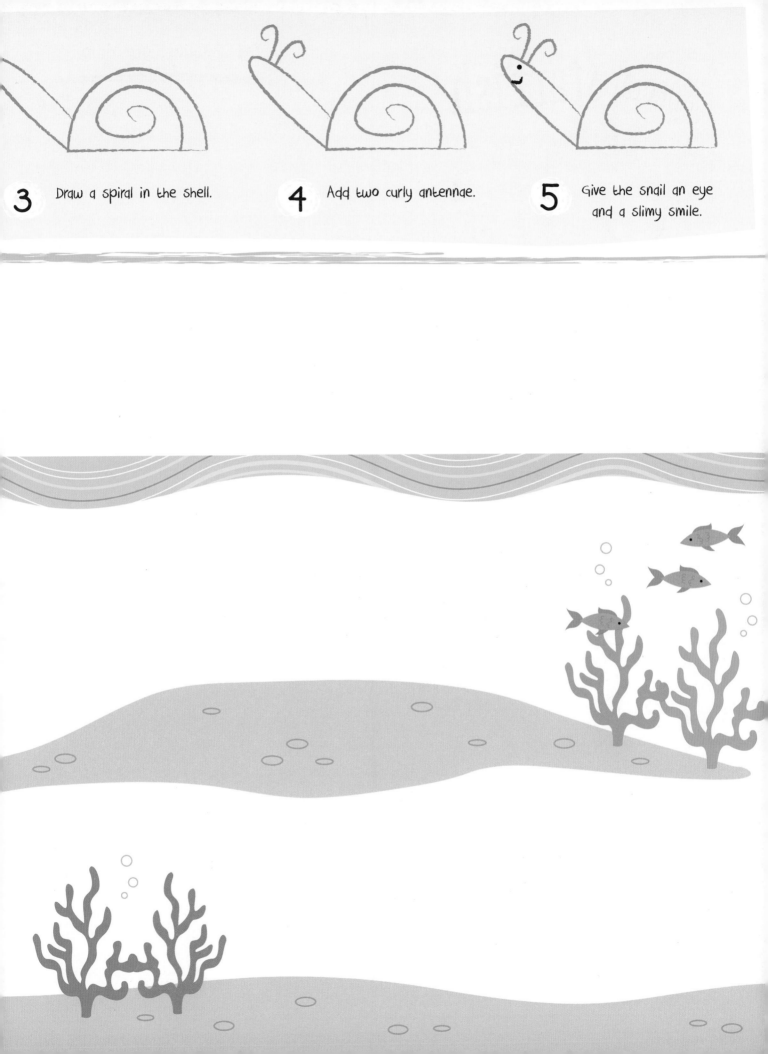

3 Draw a spiral in the shell.

4 Add two curly antennae.

5 Give the snail an eye and a slimy smile.

Special **starfish**

1

Draw a circle
for the body.

2

Add five arms.

3

Draw circles inside
the arms.

4

Give the starfish
a happy face.

Sweet **seahorses**

Try drawing your own . . .

1

Draw a circle
for the head and
add a body.

2

Add a curly line
for the tail.

3

Draw a nose
and two fins.

4

Give the seahorse a
sunny smile and add
lines on its tummy.

Jolly **jellyfish**

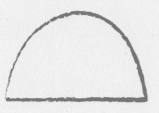

1

Draw a semicircle for the body.

2

Add lots of wiggly lines for the tentacles.

3

Give the jellyfish a jolly face.

Try drawing your own . . .

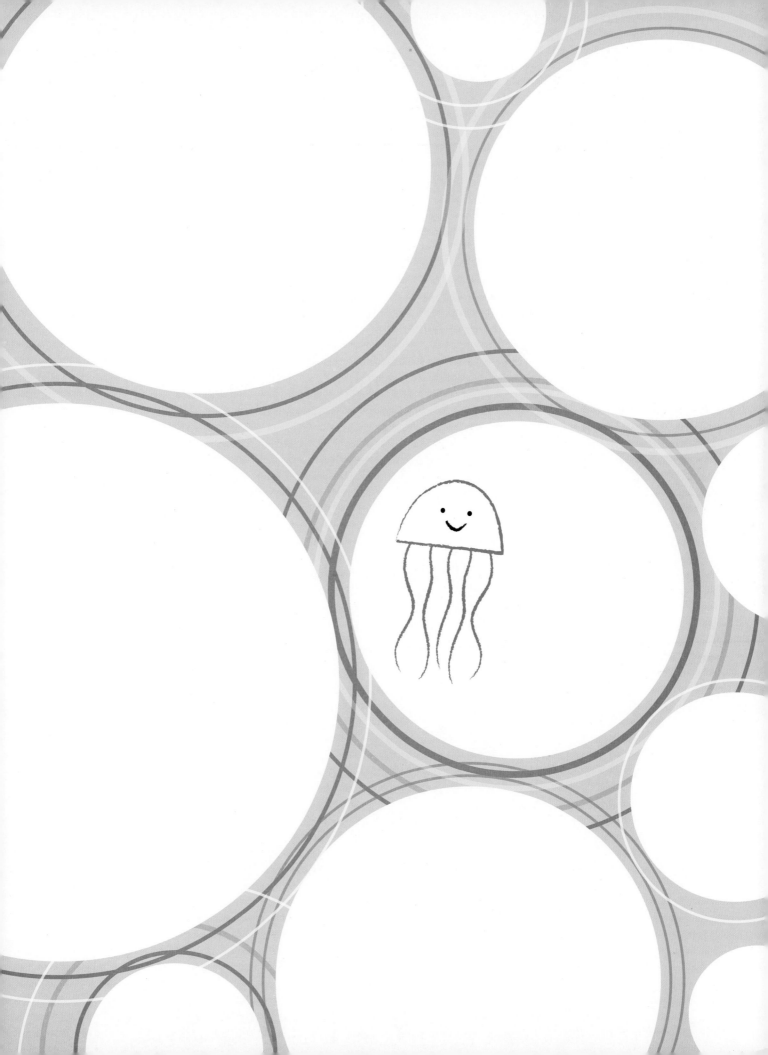

Killer whales

1 Draw a semicircle for the body.

2 Add a fin and a curved line for the tail.

Try drawing your own . . .

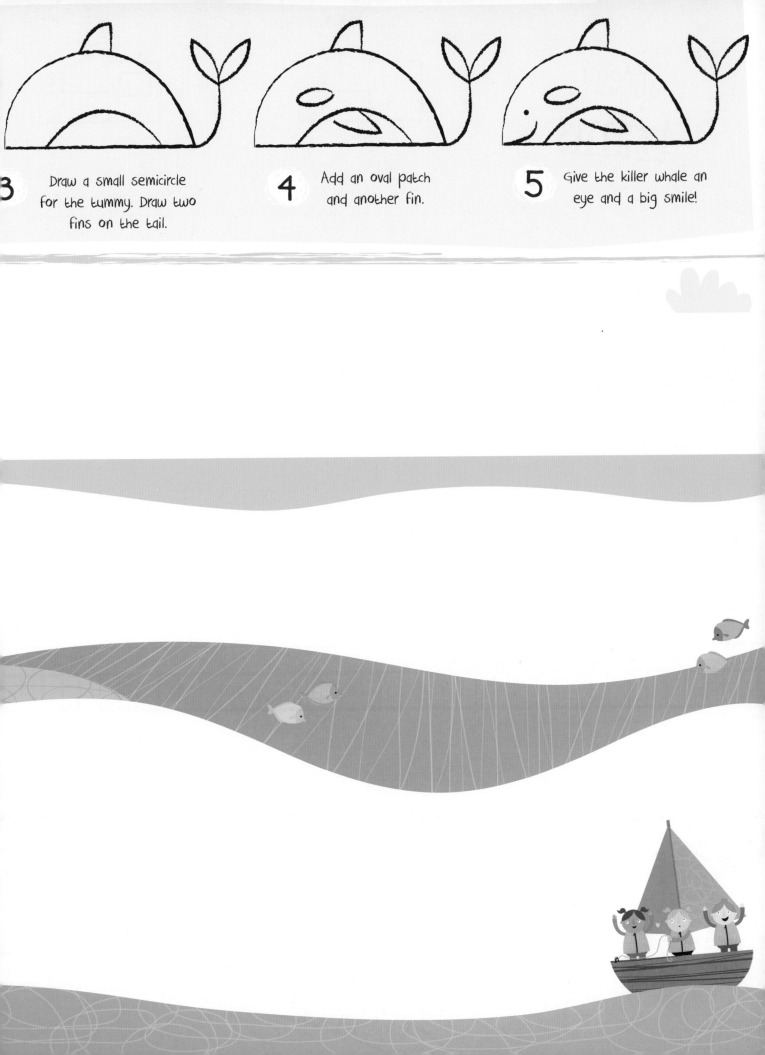

3 Draw a small semicircle for the tummy. Draw two fins on the tail.

4 Add an oval patch and another fin.

5 Give the killer whale an eye and a big smile!

Speedy trains

1 Draw a square and a rectangle for the front engine.

2 Draw a large rectangle for the window and a small rectangle for the chimney.

Try drawing your own . . .

3 Add lots of little rectangles for the cars.

4 Draw small semicircles for the wheels. Add a puff of smoke coming out of the chimney.

Super **submarines**

Try drawing your own . . .

1

Draw a big oval for the body of the submarine.

2

Add a tower.

3

Draw the propeller.

4

Add a line as the periscope and circles for the windows.

Police cars

1 Draw two circles for the wheels and a rectangle for the body of the car.

2 Draw a rectangle on top. Add a straight line down the middle for the windows.

Try drawing your own . . .

3 Add a semicircle for the siren light and two small circles in the wheels.

4 Draw lines to show the flashing light.

5 Add headlights and a stripe. Now you're ready for patrol.

Racing **rockets**

1

Draw a curved triangle for the body of the rocket.

2

Add two triangles to the bottom for the fins.

3

Draw a circle for the window.

4

Blastoff! Add some smoke.

Try drawing your own . . .

Hot-air balloons

1

Draw a circle for the balloon and add a basket.

2

Draw lines to join the basket and the balloon.

3

Decorate the balloon and basket however you want!

Try drawing your own . . .

Beautiful **boats**

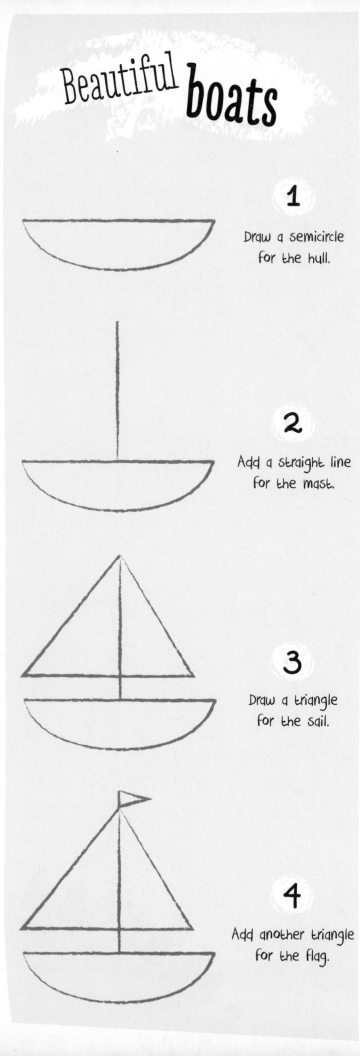

1

Draw a semicircle for the hull.

2

Add a straight line for the mast.

3

Draw a triangle for the sail.

4

Add another triangle for the flag.

Try drawing your own . . .

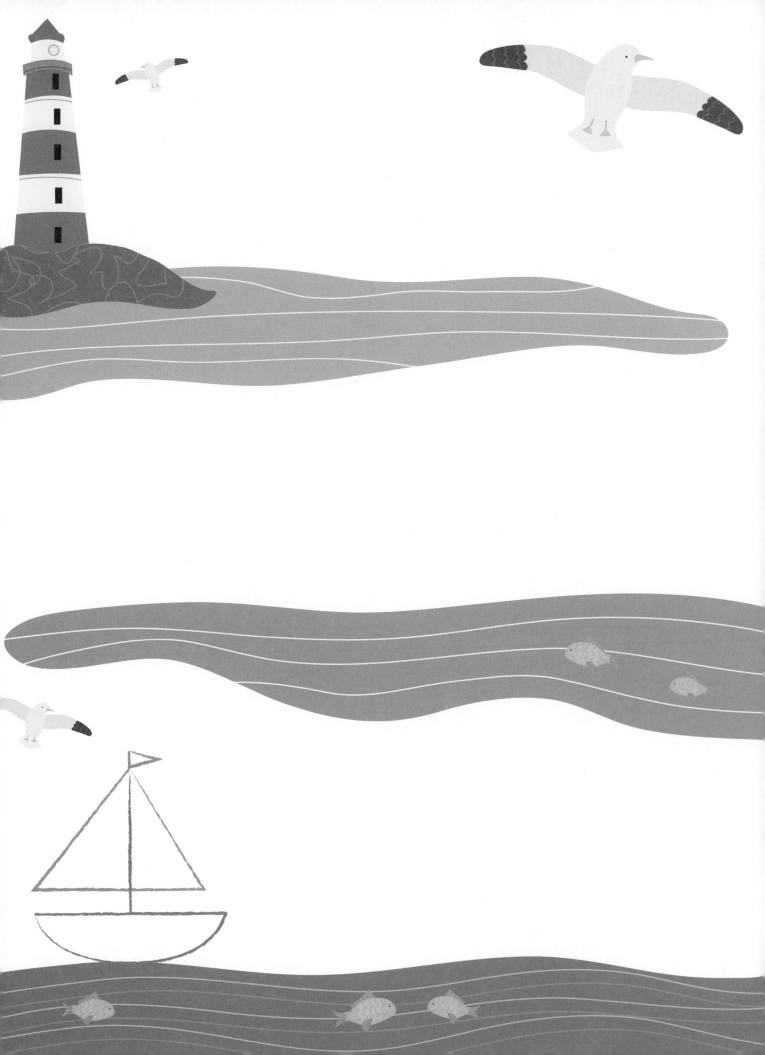

Mighty monster trucks

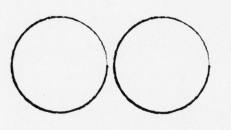

1

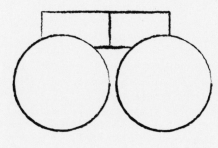

Draw two big circles for the giant wheels.

2

Draw the body of the monster truck.

3

Draw smaller circles in the wheels. Add the window frame of the truck.

4

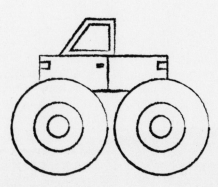

Add the window, lights, door handle, and alloy wheels.

Try drawing your own . . .

Powerful planes

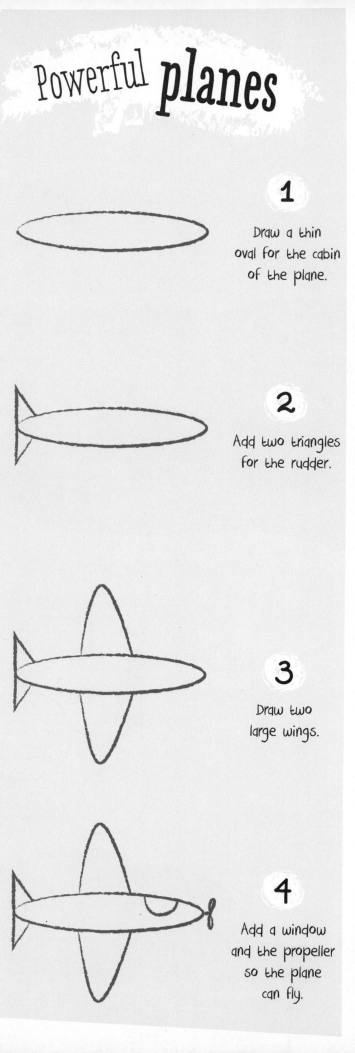

1

Draw a thin oval for the cabin of the plane.

2

Add two triangles for the rudder.

3

Draw two large wings.

4

Add a window and the propeller so the plane can fly.

Try drawing your own . . .

Humming hovercrafts

1 Draw the skirt of the hovercraft.

2 Add a tall semicircle for the propeller.

Try drawing your own . . .

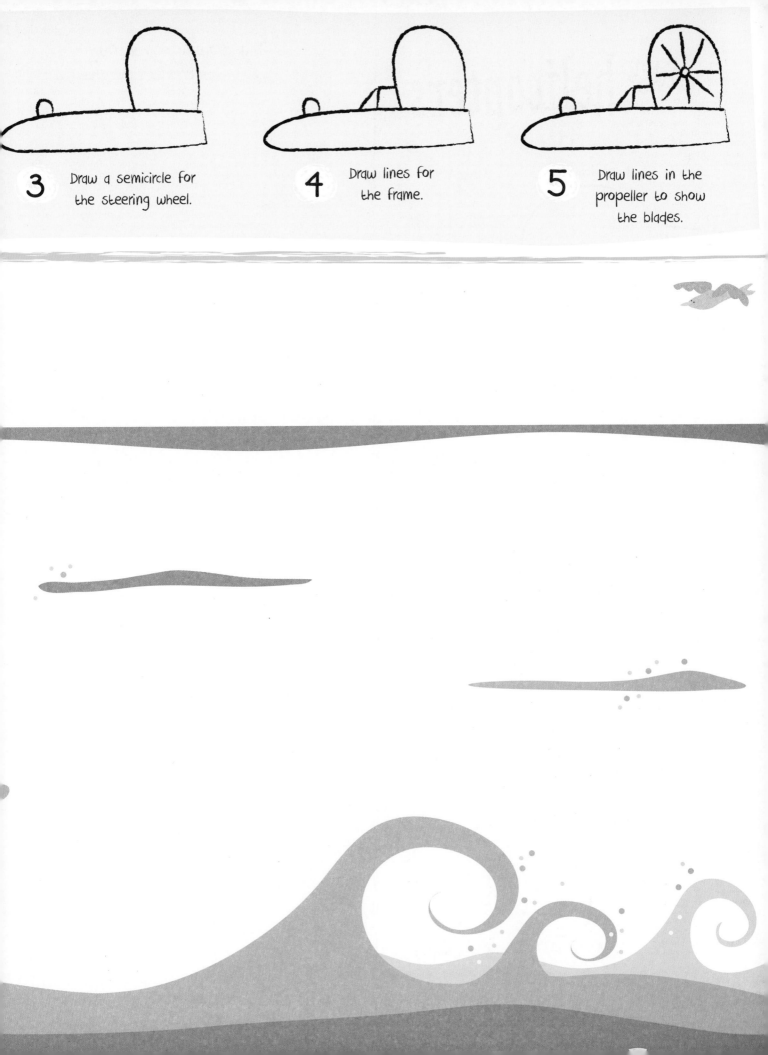

3 Draw a semicircle for the steering wheel.

4 Draw lines for the frame.

5 Draw lines in the propeller to show the blades.

Huge **helicopters**

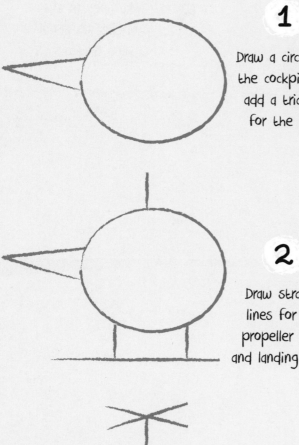

1 Draw a circle for the cockpit and add a triangle for the tail.

2 Draw straight lines for the propeller base and landing skids.

3 Add propeller blades to the roof and tail.

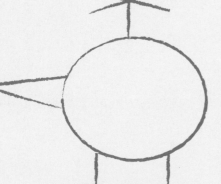

4 Add two windows. Now the helicopter can take flight!

Dangerous diggers

1 Draw the body of the digger and the tracks.

2 Add the long ar[m]

Try drawing your own . . .

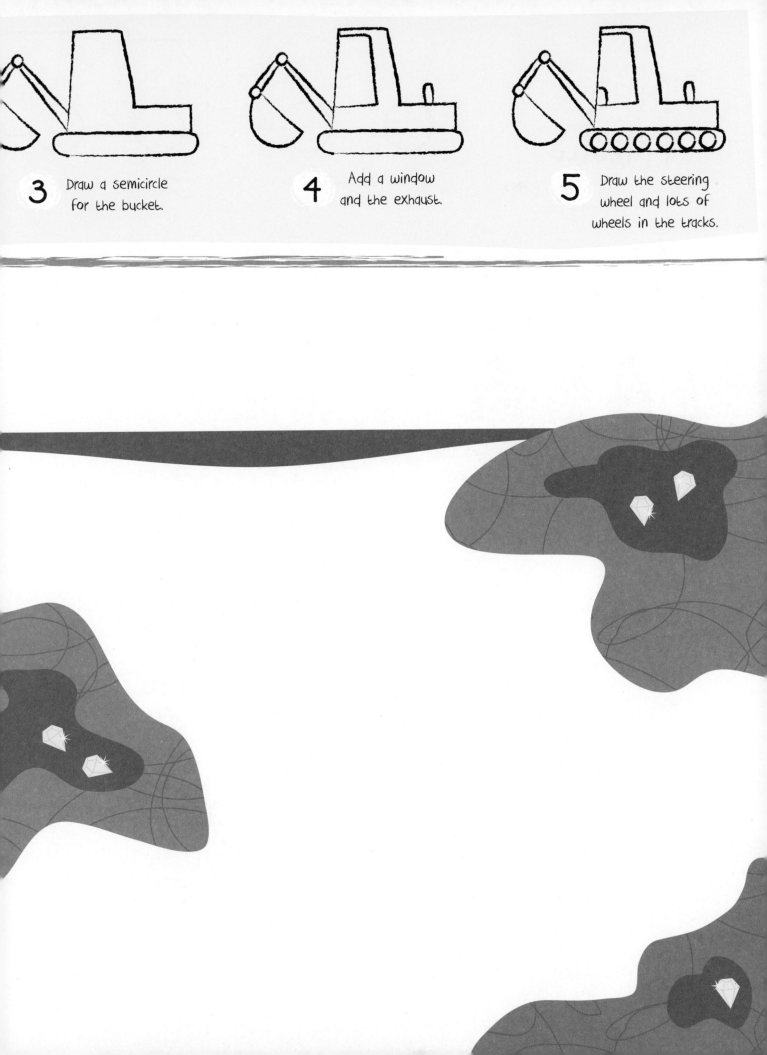

3 Draw a semicircle for the bucket.

4 Add a window and the exhaust.

5 Draw the steering wheel and lots of wheels in the tracks.

Terrific trucks

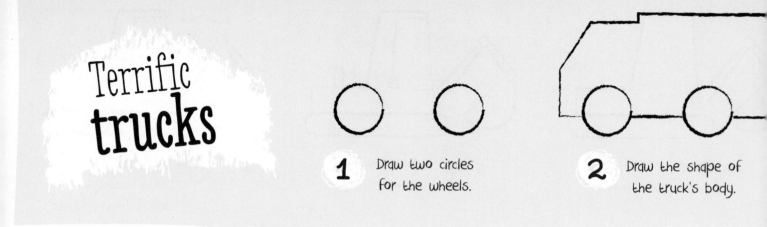

1 Draw two circles for the wheels.

2 Draw the shape of the truck's body.

Try drawing your own . . .

3 Add a window and a door.

4 Draw a line to show the trailer. Draw two small circles for the alloy wheels.

5 Draw the window, lights, exhaust, and door handle.

Drawing **faces**

Try drawing different faces on your characters to give them different moods.

Happy face

Sad face

Angry face

Surprised face

Try drawing your own . . . .

Slar

Hi

Hi

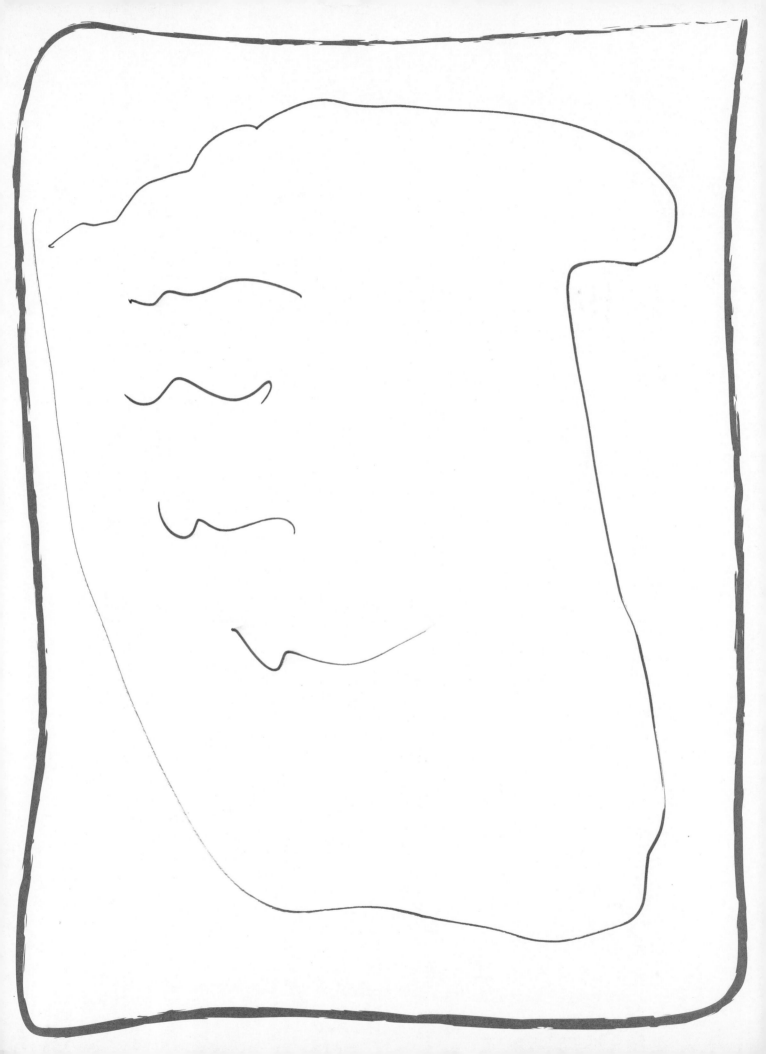

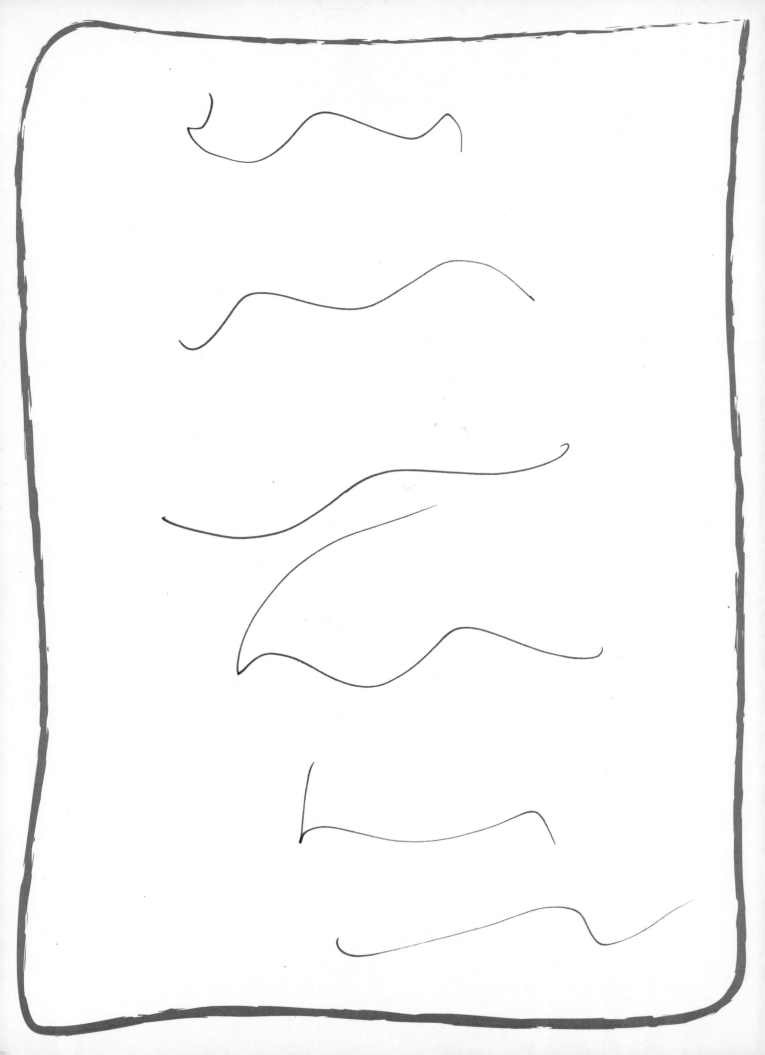